FUN FACT FILE: ENGINEERING MARVELS

20 FUN FACTS ABOUT FAMOUS RAILROADS

BY THERESE SHEA

Gareth Stevens
PUBLISHING

Please visit our website, www.garethstevens.com. For a free color catalog of all our high-quality books, call toll free 1-800-542-2595 or fax 1-877-542-2596.

Cataloging-in-Publication Data

Names: Shea, Therese.
Title: 20 fun facts about famous railroads / Therese Shea.
Description: New York : Gareth Stevens Publishing, 2020. | Series: Fun fact file: engineering marvels | Includes glossary and index.
Identifiers: ISBN 9781538246580 (pbk.) | ISBN 9781538246603 (library bound) | ISBN 9781538246597 (6 pack)
Subjects: LCSH: Railroad trains–Juvenile literature. | Railroads–Juvenile literature. | Railroad travel–Juvenile literature.
Classification: LCC TF148.S54 2020 | DDC 625.2–dc23

First Edition

Published in 2020 by
Gareth Stevens Publishing
111 East 14th Street, Suite 349
New York, NY 10003

Designer: Sarah Liddell
Editor: Therese Shea

Photo credits: Cover, p. 1 (main) Moab Republic/Shutterstock.com; file folder used throughout David Smart/Shutterstock.com; binder clip used throughout luckyraccoon/Shutterstock.com; wood grain background used throughout ARENA Creative/Shutterstock.com; p. 5 Denis Belitsky/Shutterstock.com; p. 6 saiko3p/Shutterstock.com; p. 7 John Blanton/Shutterstock.com; p. 8 CaseyMartin/Shutterstock.com; p. 9 Bardocz Peter/Shutterstock.com; p. 10 Hulton Archive/Stringer/Archive Photos/Getty Images; p. 11 Hindustan Times/Contributor/Hindustan Times/Getty Images; p. 12 Everett Historical/Shutterstock.com; p. 13 Museum of Science and Industry, Chicago/Contributor/Archive Photos/Getty Images; p. 14 Avesun/Shutterstock.com; p. 15 cyo bo/Shutterstock.com; p. 16 Kurita KAKU/Contributor/Gammo-Rapho/Getty Images; p. 17 JIJI PRESS/Contributor/AFP/Getty Images; p. 18 Majority World/Contributor/Universal Images Group/Getty Images; p. 19 Alonso de Mendoza/Wikimedia Commons; p. 20 Smith Collection/Gado/Contributor/Archive Photos/Getty Images; p. 21 George Rose/Contributor/Getty Images News/Getty Images; p. 22 FRANCOIS GUILLOT/Contributor/AFP/Getty Images; p. 23 V Kuzmishchev/Shutterstock.com; p. 24 SERGEI SUPINSKY/Contributor/AFP/Getty Images; p. 25 China Photos/Stringer/Getty Images News/Getty Images; p. 26 Oleg Kozlov/Shutterstock.com; p. 29 Ken Wolter/Shutterstock.com.

Printed in the United States of America

CPSIA compliance information: Batch #CW20GS: For further information contact Gareth Stevens, New York, New York at 1-800-542-2595.

CONTENTS

Words in the glossary appear in **bold** type the first time they are used in the text.

RAILROADS CHANGED THE WORLD

Do you know the difference between a train and a locomotive? A train is a row of cars that are linked together. It's pulled by a **vehicle** called a locomotive. Trains travel on a system of metal rails, or tracks, called a railroad.

They're common sights today, but railroads and trains changed the world after they were invented! They were an easier way to ship goods. They also helped people travel and settle in different places. Railroads, also called railways, were feats of **engineering** that shaped people's ways of life.

Railroads and trains have changed a lot since they were invented. They remain an important kind of **transportation** today.

FIRSTS

FUN FACT: 1

THE FIRST "RAILROAD" IS FROM AROUND 600 BC!

Ancient Greeks cut ruts into roads. Carts with wheels traveled in these ruts. This kind of "railroad" carried boats from one side of the Isthmus of Corinth to the other, so boats didn't have to sail around mainland Greece.

Today, a canal, or man-made waterway, cuts across the Isthmus of Corinth, allowing ships through. An isthmus is a narrow piece of land that joins two larger land areas.

FUN FACT: 2

THE FIRST RAILROAD MADE OF WOODEN TRACKS WAS LAID IN THE 1550S.

The German wooden railroad was called a wagonway. Horse-drawn wagons used it to cross the countryside. Such wagons had a hard time moving on dirt roads. Germans used wooden railroads in mines as well.

FUN FACT: 3

THE FIRST US RAILROAD COMPANY FOR CARRYING PEOPLE AND FREIGHT IS FEATURED IN THE GAME MONOPOLY!

In 1827, the Baltimore and Ohio (B&O) Railroad became the first US company to carry both passengers, or travelers, and goods. At first, it was only 13 miles (21 km) long. It later connected New York in the east to Missouri and Illinois in the west.

Of the four railroads in the original Monopoly game—the Pennsylvania, B&O, Reading, and Short Line—only the first three are real railroads!

In 1963, the Chesapeake and Ohio Railway Company bought the B&O Railroad. It later became part of the CSX company, which transports freight.

A tale is told that the Tom Thumb had a race with a horse-drawn train car. The locomotive was winning, but lost the race when a part broke.

FUN FACT: 4

THE FIRST STEAM LOCOMOTIVE BUILT IN THE UNITED STATES WAS CALLED THE TOM THUMB.

American inventor Peter Cooper built the Tom Thumb in 1830. Steam locomotives burned coal to heat water. Steam from boiling water moved machine parts that moved the locomotive. Steam-powered trains took the place of horse-drawn trains.

ALL KINDS OF TRAINS

FUN FACT: 5

IN INDIA, A STEAM LOCOMOTIVE MADE IN 1855 IS STILL ON THE JOB!

Indian Railways is the largest rail system in Asia. The Fairy Queen may be its most famous train.

The Fairy Queen is the world's oldest working steam locomotive. It stopped service in 1908, but began running again in 1997. Parts have been stolen over the years, but engineers always get it running again!

FUN FACT: 6

THE DIESEL-ELECTRIC LOCOMOTIVE CALLED THE EMD FT MADE TRAVELING THROUGH TUNNELS SAFER!

This locomotive was designed, or planned, in 1939. The motor gave off little smoke, which was helpful for train crews. In long tunnels, engine smoke made it hard to breathe!

The Moffat Tunnel through the Rocky Mountains is more than 6 miles (9.7 km) long. It was an uncomfortable ride in a steam train because of the smoke that the locomotives gave off.

The GG1 pulled both passengers and freight. It traveled over 100 miles (161 km) per hour.

FUN FACT: 7

THE GG1 ELECTRIC LOCOMOTIVE RAN IN EITHER DIRECTION—WITHOUT TURNING AROUND!

First built in 1943 for the Pennsylvania Railroad, the GG1 ran on tracks built for electric locomotives. It connected to overhead electric lines, which provided the locomotive with power.

Monorails are quick and quiet but costly to build.

FUN FACT: 8

SOME TRAINS RUN ON ONE RAIL!

Monorails are electric trains that run on or below one track. They're found in many places—including Disney parks—but only transport passengers a short way. Many are not longer than 10 miles (16 km).

TODAY'S TRAIN TECH

FUN FACT: 9

SOME TRAINS TODAY USE MAGNETS TO MOVE!

Maglev train parts last longer than those on other trains, but they can be more expensive to build. Japan, China, and Korea have maglev railways.

Maglev (or magnetic levitation) trains use **electromagnets** to lift the train off the special tracks and push the train forward. These trains look like they're levitating, or floating in the air!

FUN FACT: 10

SOME TRAINS TRAVEL FASTER THAN 350 MILES (563 KM) PER HOUR!

Technology has made very fast trains. The first steam trains moved slower than 10 miles (16 km) per hour. Trains with diesel and electric engines moved faster. The speed record today is 374 miles (602 km) per hour!

The train with the current speed record is a Japanese maglev train. Passenger trains usually travel much slower for safety reasons.

FUN FACT: 11

JAPAN HAS TRAINS SO FAST THEY'RE CALLED BULLET TRAINS!

In Japan, bullet trains are called Shinkansen. These electric-powered trains run as fast as 200 miles (322 km) per hour. A passenger bullet train called the Alfa-X will travel up to 224 miles (360 km) per hour.

TRANSCONTINENTAL TRIPS

FUN FACT: 12

THE WORLD'S LONGEST PASSENGER TRAIN PULLS 44 CARS!

The Ghan travels on a transcontinental railway, which means the tracks cross the entire **continent**.

The train called The Ghan requires two locomotives to pull it. It's about 3,600 feet (1.1 km) long, or about the length of 12 soccer fields! It carries people between the northern and southern coasts of Australia, about 1,850 miles (2,977 km).

The workers on the transcontinental railroad built tall bridges, like this one in Wyoming. Some were so quickly and poorly built that they had to be torn down and built again!

FUN FACT: 13

THE BUILDING OF THE FIRST US TRANSCONTINENTAL RAILROAD WAS A RACE!

The Pacific Railway Act of 1862 named the Central Pacific and Union Pacific Railroads as the companies to lay the tracks. The government gave the companies land and money based on the amount of track laid, so workers raced to finish!

Explosives were dangerous to handle. Workers sometimes died when they were caught in blasts.

FUN FACT: 14

TRANSCONTINENTAL RAILROAD WORKERS USED EXPLOSIVES TO CREATE TUNNELS!

Workers used explosives to build through the Sierra Nevada. In 6 years, they laid about 1,800 miles (2,897 km) of track from Nebraska to California. When connected to other railroads, it connected the West Coast and East Coast.

FUN FACT: 15

CANADA'S FIRST TRANSCONTINENTAL RAILROAD WAS COMPLETED IN 1885—6 YEARS FASTER THAN PLANNED!

People still take transcontinental train trips to enjoy Canada's beauty.

The Canadian Pacific Railway Company was founded in 1881 to build a railroad across the country. The railroad was a main reason why British Columbia agreed to join Canada when it became a **confederation**.

The Orient Express ran from 1883 to 1977 between Paris, France, and Constantinople (now Istanbul), Turkey.

FUN FACT: 16

THE ORIENT EXPRESS TRANSCONTINENTAL PASSENGER TRAIN IS FEATURED IN MOVIES AND BOOKS.

The Orient Express was known for beauty and **luxury** in a time when most trains were uncomfortable. It was featured in the books *Murder on the Orient Express* and *Dracula* as well as the James Bond movie *From Russia with Love.*

FUN FACT: 17

ONE LINE OF RUSSIA'S TRANS-SIBERIAN RAILROAD TAKES ABOUT A WEEK TO TRAVEL!

The Trans-Siberian Railroad was hard to build because the part of Russia called Siberia is cold and snowy. The railroad made settlement and business possible there.

The Trans-Siberian Railroad has one of the longest single rail lines. A passenger can go from the cities of Moscow to Vladivostok without changing trains. That's 5,778 miles (9,198 km)!

FUN FACT: 18

PART OF A TRAIN TRACK IN THE EASTERN EUROPEAN COUNTRY OF UKRAINE IS CALLED THE TUNNEL OF LOVE!

The Tunnel of Love is about 2 miles (3.2 km) long and surrounded by a natural tunnel of trees. People like to walk along it. Stories say those who visit the tunnel are granted a wish!

The trains that pass through the Tunnel of Love trim the trees by breaking the branches that stick out.

The Qinghai-Tibet Railway is the world's highest railroad! It travels through an area called "the roof of the world."

FUN FACT: 19

YOU'LL PROBABLY NEED EXTRA OXYGEN ON CHINA'S QINGHAI-TIBET RAILWAY!

The Qinghai-Tibet Railway connects northwest China and the Tibet Autonomous Region. Much of the rail line is more than 13,000 feet (4 km) above sea level, where there's less oxygen. Machines pump oxygen into the train cars!

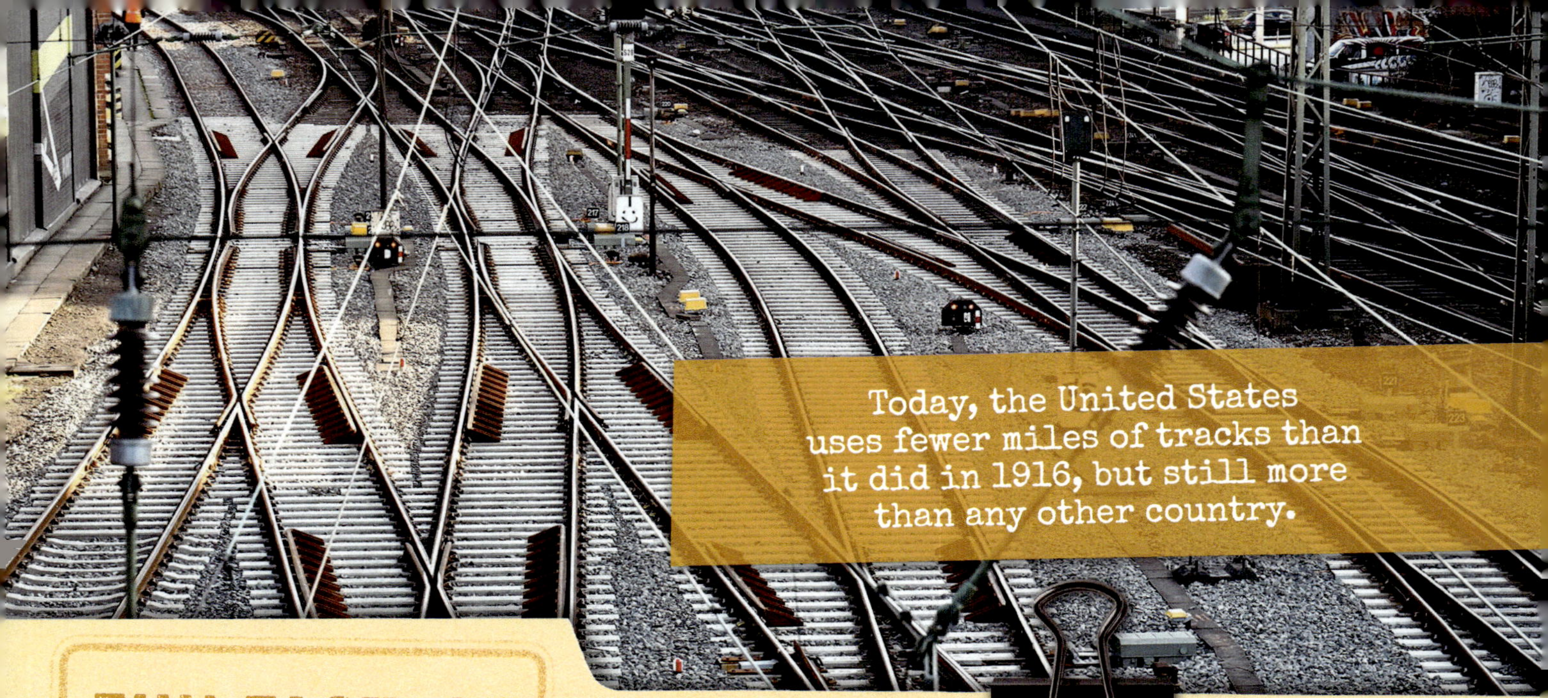

FUN FACT: 20

THE UNITED STATES HAS MORE RAILROAD TRACKS THAN ANY OTHER COUNTRY.

In 1830, the United States had 23 miles (37 km) of railroad tracks. Twenty years later, there were about 9,000 miles (14,484 km). By 1861, there were 30,000 miles (48,280 km). And in 1917, there were about 250,000 miles (402,336 km) of tracks.

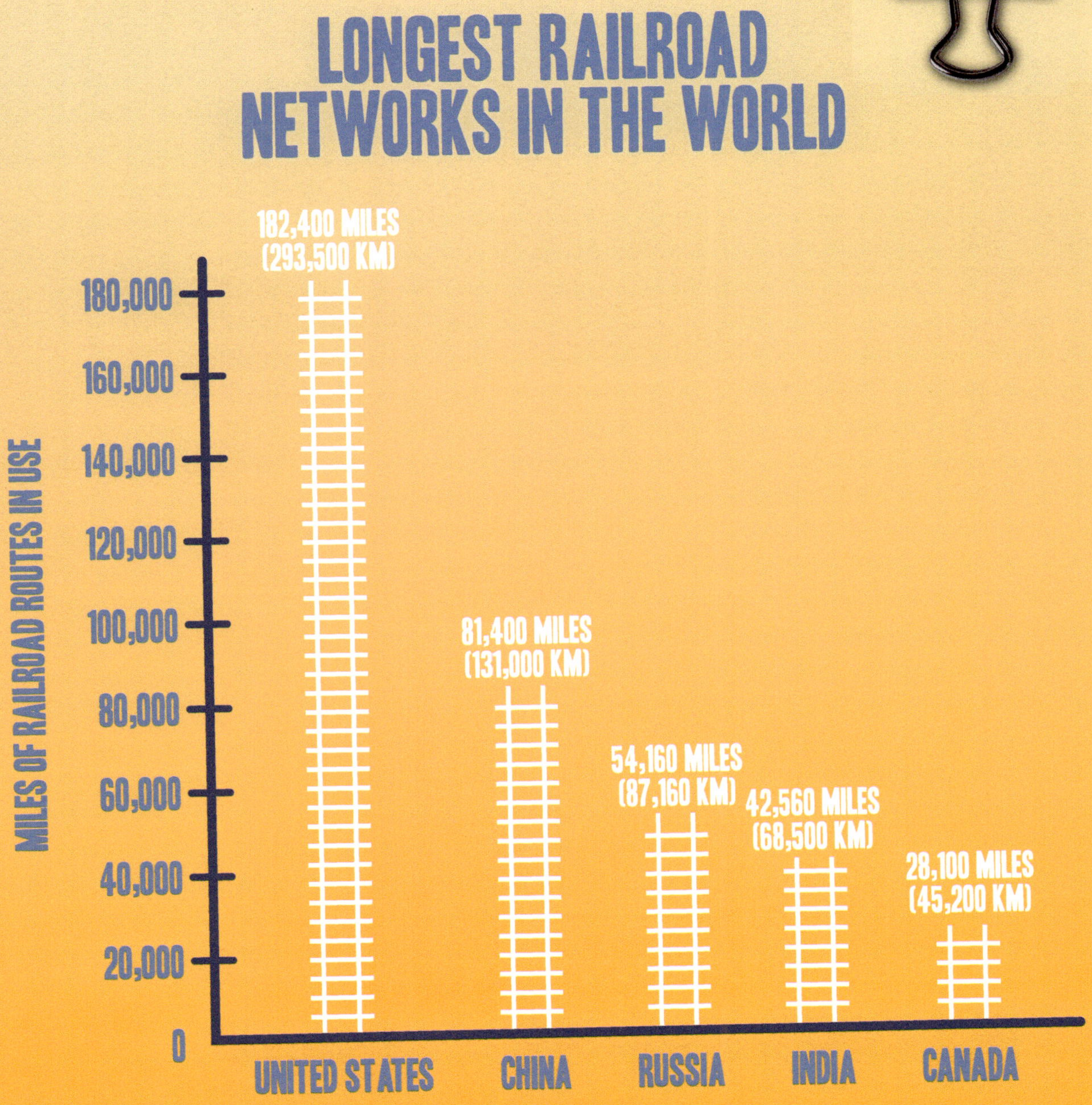

The United States uses more than twice the amount of railway track as China.

CHANGING TIMES

By the mid-1900s, fewer Americans were traveling by train. Traveling by car became common. More people traveled to faraway places by airplane. Many railroad companies went out of business. The US government began a company called Amtrak to oversee almost all passenger trains that run between cities.

While not as many Americans travel by train today, billions of dollars of freight are transported on US railways. Trains will continue to be a necessary way to travel and ship in the nation.

Many people choose to travel by rail because they think it's a pleasant way to travel—and it connects them to the great trains of the past!

GLOSSARY

bullet: a small piece of metal or other material that is shot out of a gun

confederation: a league of states that support each other and act together

continent: one of Earth's seven great landmasses

diesel: a heavy oil used as fuel in certain engines

electromagnetic: having to do with a piece of metal that becomes magnetic when electricity passes through or near it

engineering: the use of science and math to build better objects

explosive: matter used to cause a blast

freight: goods transported by ships, trains, trucks, or airplanes

luxury: something that offers more than needed and is usually more expensive

oxygen: a colorless, odorless gas that many animals, including people, need to breathe

technology: tools, machines, or ways to do things that use the latest discoveries to fix problems or meet needs

transportation: the act of moving people or things from one place to another

vehicle: an object used for carrying or transporting people or goods, such as a car, truck, airplane, or train

FOR MORE INFORMATION

BOOKS

Rivera, Andrea. *Trains*. Minneapolis, MN: Abdo Zoom, 2017.

Snedden, Robert. *Railroads*. New York, NY: PowerKids Press, 2017.

West, David. *Trains*. Mankato, MN: A+, Smart Apple Media, 2017.

WEBSITES

First Transcontinental Railroad
www.ducksters.com/history/westward_expansion/first_transcontinental_railroad.php
Read more about this incredible engineering feat.

History of Trains
www.dkfindout.com/us/transportation/history-trains/
See photos of amazing trains.

Publisher's note to educators and parents: Our editors have carefully reviewed these websites to ensure that they are suitable for students. Many websites change frequently, however, and we cannot guarantee that a site's future contents will continue to meet our high standards of quality and educational value. Be advised that students should be closely supervised whenever they access the internet.

INDEX